Prism in the Darkness

Swathi Sailesh

Presentation by *BookLeaf Publishing*

Web: www.bookleafpub.com

E-mail: info@bookleafpub.com

ISBN: 9789363311152

First edition 2024

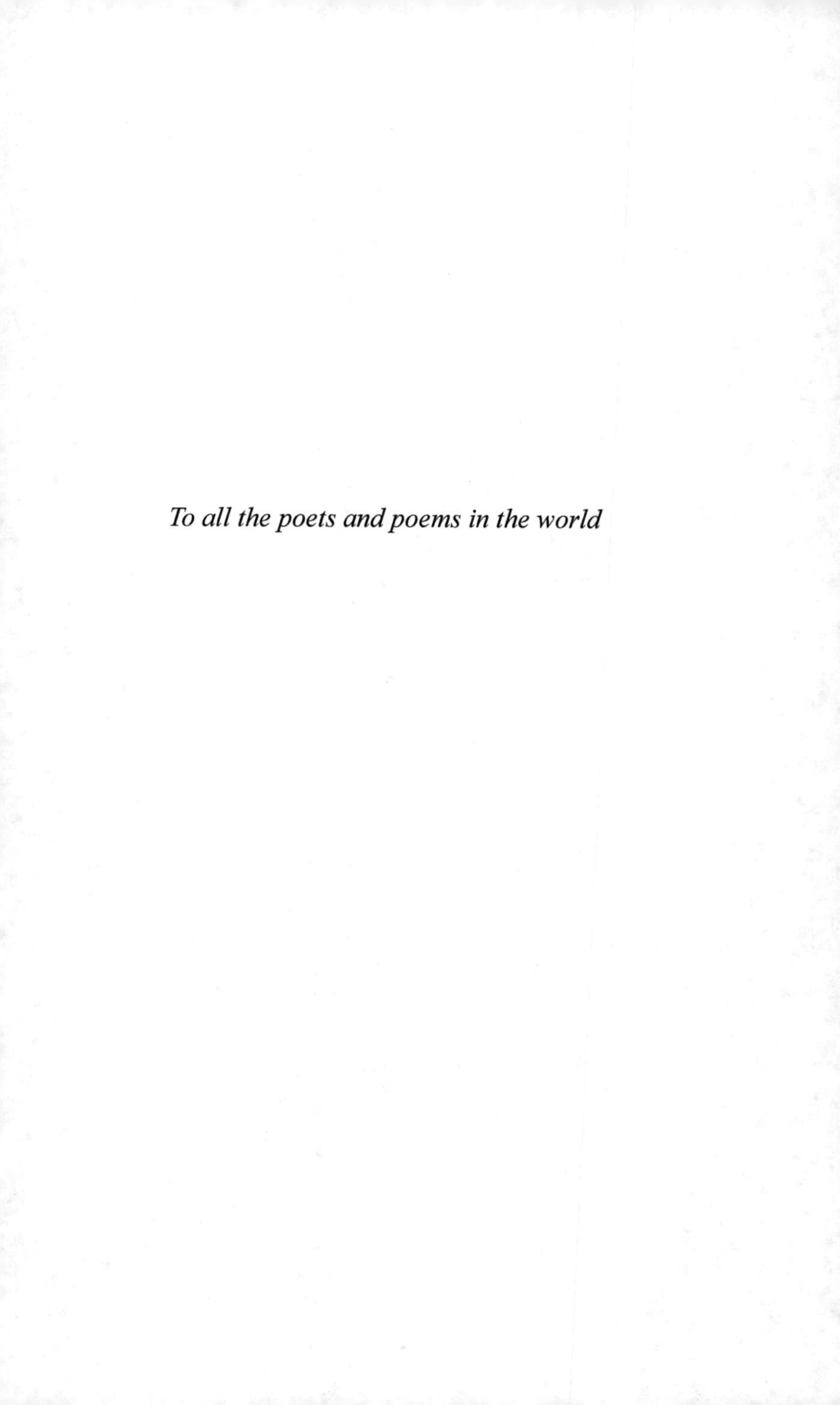

To all the poets and poems in the world

ACKNOWLEDGEMENT

I would like to thank my parents who've stood by me and my passion for writing since my childhood. I would also like to acknowledge the poets and writers who've been pivotal in my creative journey.

PREFACE

It's said that words are the truest form of magic.
There is something enchanting about a few
letters to which we have ascribed meaning
having quite so much command on our hearts.
We are fickle beings, sometimes blown by the
wind and the storms of feeling. Those words,
weighty may just hold us down. Those words
can weave webs around minds, bewitch hearts
and souls. And I feel it is a sort of duty to add
your own humble pen to this world of power and
wonderment.

 And this is something I have always believed
in. I began writing when I was very young.
Writing is more than just a hobby. It's a way of
leaving behind a physical, tangible legacy of
who you used to be at some point of time. It is a
tribute to the person you used to be, and a gift to
the person you will be.

Poetry now, what makes it so different?
Maybe because it seeks to elude. While prose
may dictate or state down facts, poetry will coat
it in a firm veneer. All that's there to be said
brims and flows beneath the surface. If prose is a
door to a vivid inner world, poetry is a frosted
window.

How much of history has been recorded in rhymes and verses? Poetry is evolving, and so is the world with it. And yet I believe that the verses we write today are nothing short of artefacts for a generation that is to come.

That is enough prose for now. It's time to open the curtain to some poetry.

Swathi
swathisailesh2008@gmail.com

TABLE OF CONTENTS

Anthill

A million of our footsteps, together surging
Can traverse not a wave of the fathomless sea
A horde of ants, building their hills
Chattering, twittering
The clouds above do not care, they stand in
proud and haughty glee
A billion anthills, precarious, slowly built
Together you pile them up
They cannot scale a meagre inch
And the mountains, they can but laugh
At this toil, at this childish folly
This mortal antidote to futility

Lost Atlantis

Leave me where lost Atlantis dreams
Throw your net into the sky
Capture the stars, weave them into tapestries
Let the waves roar, leave me beneath
These shafts of wood, so cold, insufficient
A child playing with the gods of the sea

Leave me where lost Atlantis sleeps
Leave me, cradled by the hushing waves
To depths of wakeless sleep
The song of tides and crashes
Unheard in perpetual dreams
Leave me to the blinding depths
Brilliant in their darkness
An abyss of strength, a fortress of waves
Leave me as their lonely battlements
Set our ashes afloat on dancing crests
And leave me where lost Atlantis weeps

Redeemer

You golden flower, you bird of prey
You redeeming bullet, beautiful in the light of
day
Stand against the sun and fight
There's no disgrace through all the pain
You hold hands, pale and drawn
Quiet and tear-bedimmed at the doorstep
Of death, hidden away
From the prying eyes of the world

Let them speak, whisper away
Their venomous words
You return to quiet them all
Redeemer, you have stood so tall.
Against your spirit, they gathered
But the sun comes out on top

Imperious, wherefrom do you draw your power
Nerves of steel
Veins of ice
Heart of stone
Highest of highs, lowest of lows,
In so brief a time, so much so
And you stand there, placid, beautiful
Unstoppable, a terror,
Revenge itself, in the flesh

You could do nothing wrong now
Blessed now with that covetous Midas touch
Everything you do turns to gold
Maybe at the end of it all
You can close your eyes
Proud and happier
Than the world ever thought they'd let you be
Wondering if there ever were such a thing called
euphoria
You'd feel it coursing along with the adrenaline
in your veins
Smile away now, it's your day
Your day in the sun's own gold

The Last Eclipse

Silent sky, have you swallowed the rising sun?
Mercury watches, cold, proud
The prickle of her unfamiliar eyes
Is it night? Our hearts, burgeoning
They throb with the youthful pulse of day
And yet from afar, a forlorn star
Stares upon us, maybe she remembers
The once laughing child of man

Beneath our feet, a realm of golden dust
Are those the bones of the world that was?
The ashes of all that we once loved?
Was it yesterday? Or as the world seems to
remember
An eon or so ago
Futile, our watches freeze
Humble quartz, long gone
Time, once the callous destroyer
Has ceased to have all meaning

Fretful expanse, have you robbed us of being?
We stare with wonderment
At our hands, so ageless, unweary
Are we the last men on earth?
All that is left of a hundred tales
Flowing with abundant prose
So are we the last men on earth?
Are we, are we?

Umbrella

A patch of hues against tempestuous skies
Shielding the world in its nest of lies
Breaking the path of raindrops cold
Pelting the bones of young and old
Casting away the cruel shrapnel that is ice
One cold white dagger can suffice
Icicles with that bitter chill
Guarding hearts that have not yet gone still
Casting a veil of colored light
Against the dauntlessness of night
That eerie wail of falling storm
Harbinger of truth, wordless, no form
For when drops of truth strike bare skin
The gray bleakness of the world sinks in

Summer of my Life

They say I'm in my summer
Fresh grass and shoots of green
Sun smiling brightly down
On shores awash by the sea
They believe I am a flower in bloom
Dancing in golden light
With all of life ahead of me
A future crystalline aglow

What they don't see is ceaseless sun
Beating and wearing down
Merciless power never quite done
Withered and crackled ground
They don't see you as a plant so parched
Its thorns craving for rain
Longing for respite from days
Of plodding through endless pain

They see lustre and golden shine
They see a life so radiant
All they see is a happy bud
Scrounging for love and light
They don't see the shriveled seed
They see not the rivers dry
All they see is the clear blue glow
Of the cloudless sky

What is a dream?

What is a dream?
A single painting
Frosted, glazed and so sweetly filled
With the silent periwinkles of May
Dreams, some bloom like a summer blossom
Dainty rainbows against rain drenched feet
Blurring in an incandescent haze
Such is a dream to me, a fairytale

What is a dream ?
A fearful dawn
Lightning against blood born sky
Harkening, the world takes cover
Crouches against the night black ledge
Formed of ice, carved of fear
An ember of endless flame fades away
Into the waiting shadows, for what is a dream?
But a nightmare gone wrong

What is a dream?
If not an old, old rose
Pressed against the malignant pages
Of time itself, callous destroyer
Sweet and sour, shades of yesterday
I call upon them in dreams

Don't go, I plead
For a dream is the only place memories can
breathe
But dawn is coming, and the night must end
Among all these sepia shades, I painted myself
The winds of time are howling
The pages of history are turning
The clock is a Memento Mori
Against the wall
And such is a dream, a silhouette of a memory
We humans cannot leave

Man in the Mirror

So who are you then? Beneath it all
Away from the flashy lights
And all the ringmarole of the world
What is it then that you believe in?
That pushes out that golden smile
And when you're alone, somewhere in faraway
loneliness
Does the glare of their eyes ever seem
It could burn you down ?

Somewhere they whisper your name
Hail you the hero, the deliverer
The one with eyes as blue as the seas of the
faraway south
They shall remember your name
In fervour, in the pages of history
The camera frames, still with your faded smile
It's the smile of a dream come true

They throng, they say that they love you
But do they even know?
The nerves beneath those reflexes, the heart
behind that snow?
Only you can see the cinders, left from the
bonfires of youth

The blue eyed boy once picking the pebbles
Staring at the rocks that now bear your name
So the legend on a hundred paper covers
Is the sombre man, staring into the mirror, wondering
Who he was and who he used to be
Before and beyond the bend of glass, the silhouettes pressing in
Flashing with the longing eyes of the world

To Be Alone

Who knew what it's like
To be alone
To stand sole in bustling crowds
To have noone to look at you twice
To be invisible for life
To see the flowers grow in silent spring
Trodden on, trampled before they had a chance
To bloom, to become, to begin
To feel the pulse of the world, as one
And your own, discordant
To be the single chord that does not resonate
With the myriad symphonies of the orchestra
To walk down the road, with the sun in your
eyes
No echo of footsteps behind you
To not have anyone to give a knowing smile
To truly dwell alone
To see the stars that sadly glow
Wordlessly without constellations
To see the birds at twilight still
Shrouded by the willows, they too are alone
To see the swell of life and the surge of crowds
The laughter ringing off the dreary walls
Who knew that the saddest you'll feel
Will always be in a crowd

La Niña

You're everywhere, you chase
You remember me , you wait
You crouch behind me
You follow me in a drift of wind
The elegies I hear you sing
Churning up the El Nino
I turn to see you as you fly
I open the door, and in a heartless gale
You whispering rush out

You are the ghost of my yesterdays
A spectre from days long past
You are a page of a diary torn
And ripped apart by hungry crows
On a summer day, decades long last
You speak to me of mistakes made,
of fears
So true, yet so false, they came to words

You with your childish laughter
You with your wilful, derisive smile
You with your vibgyor spectrum
That haunts me in shades of gray
You hunt me down, you elude me
You turn the silent slumbering air
Into a kaleidoscope of fear
You are the memory of a girl
Who once laughed
And does no more

The Climbing Perch

Can we call ourselves free?
When a thousand innocent feathers are swept
away
From the floor of the slaughterhouse
So that's who we are, the last souls on earth
The descendents of a generation that knew its
voice
Where has our rage gone?
Faded into the winds of unprotesting compliance
And so are we the fishes who are made to climb
trees?
And if we were after all to speak
Who shall hear the yodel of youth, strong even
as he flails?
Who wants to hear the plaintive bleating of the
inmates of the slaughterhouse?
Dispensable cogs in a broken machine
There's piety in knowledge
Not in desecration
So we writhe and the venom sweeps in through
our gills
As we figure too late
The sky never was ours to claim
And from the forest floor is swept away
The rainbows glinting off our scales
The fishes who tried to climb the trees

The Princess in the Tower

They talk about the princess in the tower
Patient and penitent and sweet
Her smile of love and her song of sorrow
Her whispers to her gallant lover
They talk about him, as a hero
As the knight who held the bridge
Who fought for the princess in the tower
As she sat weaving Penelope's yarns
Until he was victorious, but fallen down
They call him brave when he answered the call
 Call her sweet when she sang of his loss
Never called her brave for being the one alone
Never called her brave for waiting in the tower
For being the one the sacrifice was for

They speak of his courage to lift up the dagger
To draw the sword, lay out doom and fire
To lay pale and still, with a smile of a lover
Knowing he died for the princess in the tower
And what of them who silent wonder
Of what her eyes see when they take in another
day
Who take her silence for a heart very much
Alive through the flames of a funeral pyre

Never dream of setting a crown afire
Never speak of her sacrifice as she blankly
gazes,
Chords of eternal regret
Tucked in a mourner's song
She's never to know the jubilance of diving into
fire
Burn with the world, that you set ablaze
What could the world, a parting gift of pain
Ever have to offer, in his death
Knowing he died for her, the princess in the
tower
A spirit locked in the pages of a fairytale

The World's Gone Quiet

So I believe
In the rousing cheers and fairy lights
That victory is sketched in my destiny
The sun smiles on me, a celestial benefactor
That this is what the stars have ordained
When they tossed in their midnight reverie
I feel the love, blooming like a million roses
Under my now bleeding feet

So I believe
And walk my way to hysteria
Of screaming crowds
Who believed it was supposed to be
All that is heard is a falling drop
Of rain, from red rimmed eyes
It's so quiet, the world's gone quiet

The sky is beautiful and clear
No hint of thunder or black clouds to rain
Not on my parade but on my dirge
Wind not howling, skies are flawless gray
Roses nothing but corsages on a coffin's
shadowed way
Dirge too gone, the world's gone quiet

It is lonely at the almost-top
Echo around me the falling swish
Of a million shattered dreams
The journey so beautiful, I remember
Without a smile
The destination was grisly gray
So I live,
Through the cheery declamations
Waiting for the thunder to crash and the resilient
world to break
You can't hear that. There's no rain
The world's gone quiet

Girls Like Me

Girls like me, we spend our days
Shifting horizons, grasping out for stars we
cannot reach
We strive to fathom
The unfathomable, push limits
The weight of the world on our shoulders
The gilt of a hundred trophies
Sleeping innocent on showcases at home
Our eyes flash at night
With words and numbers that dictate
So much more than they ought to do

Girls like me, we feel wrath, pain, we never
truly know
The world beyond a sheaf of rustling answer
sheets
For our dreams are teeming
With the scorching blaze of being number two
We, like fate, stretch out our arms
In the weighing of the scales
We glance at boards, we shiver, we fear, we
envy
Easy hearts, hands that never shake, tears that
never fall

For only when you've always had it
Are you closest to losing it all
And the loftier the fortress tower
The worse is the free fall
So for girls like me, in every victory
In one way or the other, we always lose

Forever Sixteen

I wonder if time has picked up its knives
And started carving you yet, for you seem
To be against everything it stands for
Strange to belive that somewhere in the world
People know you as such, weathered
To me it seems improbable you ever could be
Anything but forever sixteen

Sixteen, as pretty as the first ray of dancing
dawn
I wonder if your light has hastened to dusk yet ,
as has mine
Somehow I still believe you to be a fly in amber
Beating butterfly wings
Frozen on the threshold of time
Somewhere in yesterdays of mine, forever
sixteen

I wonder if you have caught all the stars in the
sky
In the net you always were weaving
For it seems strange to think of you
As anything but still spinning out its yarn

Have the shadows melted into you ?
As they melted into me all those years hence
Will you join me yet, stars and all?
For we'll both be forever sixteen again
You with the stars in your net
And me with nothing but hollow mourning
songs
Sung for you but not for me
You in a marble tomb and me in my pauper
grave
Cold feet under
Damp ground above
Forever sixteen

Letter to a Little Flower

You bloom, slender shaft
Pirouette of red blossoms
Sweet and small, rocked to sleep
By the cradle of the great green arms
In silent wonderment, you flail in the breeze
Dreaming of the great world beyond
Crawl back in, I wish you could

Far off, where your young petals don't reach
There's discordant clashes of sword
There's ice cold frost spreading its arms
Lovingly around silent hearts,
There's a sky thats gray, a world that hates
And somewhere, to you, far far away,
There's a world that doesn't want life anymore
Can you take the blaze of a hundred fires?
That can singe your sweet rouged petals right
off?
Can you feel the ebbing pulse of a world?
That once used to love, and no longer does
Crawl back in, return to that dreamless ether
The world will only trod and crush you down

The Son of the Sun

She stares through her golden eyelids
Sweetness in patient bearing
For she has seen in her own journey
Across the finger-painted skies
She has seen the fiery man rise
Race across, hide in caves
The fear of the stumbling prey in his eyes
She's seen him rise in flints and flames
A infinitesimal thread of her precious rays
She's seen him grow, she's watched him over
As a blossoming child

She's seen green fields, ripe by his hands
And she's shielded her eyes
Averted from the blood
On the hands of her unconditional son
Seen her bounty put to waste
By the clash of sword in heartless haste
Day after day, breaking like herself
Through the thunderous ignorant clouds

Whats there for her? She's faded in yore
Curious numbed, as horrors unfold
Mushroom clouds and bullet stings
And in her sorry slumber she wordless waits
For a hastening light stronger than her pain
To envelop her, and her immortal child
In its voluptuous oblivion of an embrace

All those Winter Days

All those winter days
They won't believe I learnt so much
In all those hours
Wracking us in frigidity
Shivering in its restless breath
For it won't leave you, try as you may
Until you turn to yet another flake
In the heart of the blizzard

Noone sees the pain that clouds
Those limpid wooden eyes
Noone sees the hate that cracks
The sirens that embrace us
Barren souls as the icicles blow
All those winter days

Then those old diaries we read
Flipping in the pits of memory
The dreams that were dreamt
The few instances of summer touch
In that November haze
Waiting, waiting, destitute
Quite alone in the world
Stretched out on the rack, we lay
Somehow we were pricked
By every needle we sought
In that glacial haystack

They couldn't see us as marionettes
Of that invisible puppet string
In all those winter days as we
Ached for a beginning
When those glaciers melted
We trod uncertain, learning,
Yet again, how to breathe

The Squabble?

Waltzing, dancing in the face of death
With a vigour that does naught but encompass
An eternity of last breaths
Staring gallantly into reddened eyes
Laughing in the face of the destroyer
Indifferent obedience with hearts of ice
Minds chilling with wordless dread
Fierce echoes of poison green
Creeping over fields stained red
For this is war, and this isn't fair
And there is nothing good to be seen there

For there is blood on the roses
There is hellfire stretched
There is a bitter lesson sought in stone
In these memories to be etched
They stand around a shattered tower
The ruin that yet echoes
The venomous screech of revenge
Amplified by their death throes

They are playing now, a pointless game
Played years ago in the selfsame fields
Where the nameless now lay
Why do they
For this is war and this isn't fair
There is nothing good to be seen there

Oh you Victor!

Once upon a better day
I stood right where you are now
I was the Victor, standing tall
Proving to the world what was my worth
Do you think I don't understand
What it feels like to be so powerful
With the world at my command?
Do you count me among the millions?
Clapping unknown in a trance
Surely even you remember
My very same victory dance?

Oh you Victor!
Take this chance
Rejoice with the teeming masses
Who even now, clapping so hard
Will not cast you a second glance
Surely you cannot believe ?
That your time as the crowning jewel
The roses, the adulation
Ever could come to an end
I have been there and back
And trust me, it is not fair
Surely I feel longing too
But it's harder when you've once been there

Oh you Victor!
Take this as a warn
Remember me on the day you wake
Up to a cloudless morn
Now you cannot see
Drunk with that sweetest victory wine
Perhaps you even think I despise you
As I rightfully should
But on the day that you are forsaken
As the world hounds around its newest prince
At one corner of the globe, silent
Remember me you would

One day you shall plummet deep deep down
And then we both will have lost our crown

Swan Song

The sun comes down on empty grass
The world turns round and round
Pushing out these cold blooded tides
Of long strung words, I now fail to comprehend
Wrenched in ash from the daily stash
Words that cannot be burned away
Without it who am I?
My world says I'm a disgrace
They hound at my doorstep while I lock the
gates

Should have walked away when I could
Couldn't just do the easy thing
Wait for the tides to take the sand away
Walk away when they thought I would
And here I am, all those days later
The instrumentalists all frozen
The shaking chords
Is this a swan song?